Breaking Barriers, Defying Expectations, a

Breaking Barriers, Defying Expectations, and Inspiring Generations

The Robert De Niro Story,

By

Samantha B. Steward

Breaking Barriers, Defying Expectations, and Inspiring Generations

All rights reserved. Except for brief quotations included in critical reviews and certain other noncommercial uses allowed by copyright law, no part of this publication may be reproduced, distributed, or transmitted in any form or by any means, including photocopying, recording, or other electronic or mechanical methods, without the publisher's prior written permission.

Copyright (2023) by Samantha B. Steward.

Preface

Few figures in the history of film history are as respected and revered as Robert De Niro. De Niro is an actor whose skill cuts across genres and decades. His rise from the streets of New York to the top of Hollywood is proof of the value of perseverance, adaptability, and a strong devotion to one's work. The biography *"Breaking Barriers, Defying Expectations, and Inspiring Generations: The Robert De Niro Story"* goes into the life and career of this remarkable person, whose influence on the film industry is both long-lasting and deep.

This book explores the many facets of De Niro's profession, following his journey from his early years to his ascent to become a worldwide celebrity. It looks at the key events that molded his career path, such as his innovative partnerships with renowned

Breaking Barriers, Defying Expectations, and Inspiring Generations

filmmakers and his bold attitude to playing a wide range of roles. By means of painstaking investigation and perceptive evaluation, we unearth the mysteries of De Niro's method acting, his revolutionary role preparations, and the creative decisions that distinguish him in a talent-filled field.

The impact of Robert De Niro goes beyond the big screen. His business endeavors, which include starting the Tribeca Film Festival, are a testament to his strong belief in encouraging innovation and helping up-and-coming artists. His charitable work and advocacy show that he is committed to leveraging his position to further good deeds and change the world.

This book sheds insight on De Niro's personal background as well as the memorable parts he has played. It looks at his family life, upbringing, and the difficulties he encountered in both his personal and professional life. Our goal is to bring readers a thorough knowledge of Robert De Niro's motivations, both as an artist and as a person, by offering a complete picture of his life.

"Breaking Barriers, Defying Expectations, and Inspiring Generations" pays tribute to the spirit of tenacity, the pursuit of greatness, and the bravery to defy expectations in addition to celebrating De Niro's remarkable career. We are reminded of the timeless principles his path teaches—lessons about perseverance, honesty, and the unwavering pursuit of one's passion—as we go through the many phases of his life and work.

My sincere appreciation goes out to all the people who helped make this book possible. It pays tribute to the legacy of a real movie great.

By providing readers with an insight into the remarkable life of a man who has had a lasting impression on the film industry, *"Breaking Barriers, Defying Expectations, and Inspiring Generations: The Robert De Niro Story"* is my goal that it will both inspire and educate them. I hope Robert De Niro's narrative captivates and inspires you as much as it has me as you flip these pages.

We are grateful that you have joined us on this adventure.

Sincerely,

Samantha B. Steward

Breaking Barriers, Defying Expectations, and Inspiring Generations

Table of Content

Chapter 1
New York City Upbringing
Finding Your Acting Passion
Mentors and Family as Influences
Hollywood Breakthrough

Chapter 2
Mean Streets and Scorsese
Making an Icon as a Taxi Driver
Changing to Fit a Part
The Acting Methods of Robert De Niro

Chapter 3
A Performance That Defines a Career
A Dynamic Pair
Oscar Winning
A Bronx Tale, De Niro's Directorial Debut

Chapter 4
Comedy Exploration
Getting Ready for Your Role

Philanthropy and Entrepreneurial Activities
Handling the Personal and Workplace

Chapter 5
A Durable Legacy of Impact on American Cinema
Effects Internationally
Robert De Niro's Political Voice
Getting Past Obstacles

Chapter 6
Fatherhood and Family
Examining Various Genres
Evolution and Adaptability for a Long-Term Career
Molding the Next Generation

Chapter 7
Character Development as an Art
Collaboration with Masterful Directors
Outstanding Acts of the Twenty-First Century

Breaking Barriers, Defying Expectations, and Inspiring Generations

Chapter 8
Acquiring Knowledge from a Living Myth
Robert De Niro's Enduring Impact
Food for thought
Acknowledgement

Introduction

Robert De Niro is an institution rather than just an actor. His name is a byword for outstanding filmmaking, unwavering commitment, and career-changing performances. We must first comprehend the fundamental components that have led to his legendary stature in the film business before we can begin to explore his illustrious career. This introduction provides an overview of De Niro's life, career, and lasting influence and provides insight into what makes him one of Hollywood's most admired characters.

August 17, 1943, saw the birth of Robert Anthony De Niro Jr. in New York City. His early exposure to the arts was undoubtedly affected by the fact that both of his parents, Virginia Admiral and Robert De Niro Sr., were well-known painters. De Niro was raised in the thriving cultural environment of Greenwich Village, where he was exposed to creative expression and creativity from an early age. It was in this setting that he developed a passion for acting, which would later make him a global celebrity.

New York City theaters served as the starting point in De Niro's voyage to Hollywood. His early acting endeavors were characterized by an unwavering dedication to perfecting his trade. He began studying the method acting style that would become his trademark at the Stella Adler Conservatory and then at Lee Strasberg's Actors Studio. The approach, which prioritizes a profound psychological integration into a character, enabled De Niro to imbue his performances with an

Breaking Barriers, Defying Expectations, and Inspiring Generations

unmatched degree of genuineness and passion.

Acting as a terminally sick baseball player, he made his feature film debut in "Bang the Drum Slowly" (1973). With her performance, which won praise from critics, De Niro demonstrated her capacity to portray sensitivity and intense emotion. But what really propelled him to the top of American film was his partnership with director Martin Scorsese. De Niro's depiction of the impulsive and erratic Johnny Boy in "Mean Streets" (1973) laid the groundwork for a string of legendary parts that would come to define his career.

One of the most renowned partnerships in movie history is that of De Niro and Scorsese. Collectively, they produced a body of work that reinterpreted the gangster genre while simultaneously pushing the frontiers of narrative. Their creative collaboration is evident in films like

"Goodfellas" (1990), "Raging Bull" (1980), and "Taxi Driver" (1976). De Niro won several honors, including *two Academy Awards for Best Actor*, and received critical praise for his depiction of nuanced, sometimes disturbed characters in these movies.

One especially notable aspect of "Taxi Driver" is De Niro's transition into Travis Bickle, a deluded Vietnam War veteran on the verge of insanity. De Niro's famous improvised phrase, "You talkin' to me?" has been ingrained in popular culture, signifying the actor's capacity to fully embrace his roles. This part showcased his bravery in taking on difficult and contentious themes, a quality that has characterized a large portion of his career.

In *"Raging Bull,"* De Niro demonstrated an unprecedented level of commitment to his art. He undertook a physical makeover to accurately represent boxer Jake LaMotta.

This entailed intense training to reach peak physical condition and then gaining a large amount of weight to represent LaMotta's latter years. His reputation as one of the most devoted performers of his time was cemented by his Academy Award for Best Actor, which he received for his dedication to realism.

The influence of De Niro on film goes beyond his iconic roles. He was a key figure in the revitalization of lower Manhattan and the promotion of independent cinema as one of the founders of the Tribeca cinema Festival. Founded in the aftermath of the September 11 attacks, the festival has grown to be a major cultural occasion that promotes a feeling of camaraderie among those working in the film business and showcases up-and-coming talent.

De Niro has shown to have a remarkable aptitude to transition between different parts and genres throughout his career. His

Breaking Barriers, Defying Expectations, and Inspiring Generations

variety of work is seen in his flexibility, which spans from the serious dramas of his early career to the humorous performances in movies like *"The Intern"* (2015) and *"Meet the Parents"* (2000). His dedication to quality has not wavered throughout the years, even if his duties have changed.

De Niro's reputation has been further solidified by his commitment to social and political concerns and his honesty, in addition to his accomplishments on film. His platform has been used to promote a wide range of causes, from governmental transparency to creative freedom, demonstrating his steadfast conviction in utilizing his power for the greater good.

In the chapters that follow, we will go further into Robert De Niro's life and career, examining the subtleties of his playing style, the complexities of his most well-known parts, and the life events that influenced him. "Breaking Barriers, Defying

Expectations, and Inspiring Generations" seeks to provide readers a thorough grasp of the guy who is behind the legend as well as the actor. This biography provides insightful information on the characteristics of genuine creative genius and the unwavering quest of excellence that has motivated countless numbers of people.

Chapter 1

New York City Upbringing

Robert De Niro was born on August 17, 1943, in New York City's thriving and culturally diverse Greenwich Village area. This is where his tale starts. This chapter explores his early experiences and influences, which helped to build the basis of his remarkable career.

Robert Anthony De Niro Jr. was raised by two parents who were artists, and their influence on him will never fade. His mother, Virginia Admiral, was a painter and poet, and his father, Robert De Niro Sr., was an abstract expressionist painter and sculptor. Because the family was heavily involved in the arts, young Robert had an early affinity for expression and creativity.

In the 1940s and 1950s, De Niro grew up in Greenwich Village, surrounded by a vibrant community of authors, musicians, and painters. It is impossible to overestimate the impact of this free-spirited community on De Niro's early years. It was a center of cultural activity. De Niro gained a distinct outlook on life and the arts from the diverse neighborhood, which was renowned for its progressive and avant-garde vibe. This gave him a strong feeling of creative inquiry.

Even in the ostensibly perfect creative setting, De Niro had difficulties as a young kid. His family dynamic was complicated by the fact that his parents divorced when he was only two years old. Although De Niro spent most of his time with his mother, his father continued to play a big role in his life. De Niro had to go through a time of psychological turmoil as a result of the split and the ensuing family arrangements, but he also gained resilience and independence that would help him in his future career.

Breaking Barriers, Defying Expectations, and Inspiring Generations

Due to his family's rather unusual parenting style, De Niro had his early schooling in a succession of schools. He went to the Little Red School House, Elisabeth Irwin High School, Public School 41 in Greenwich Village, and finally the High School of Music & Art in New York. But De Niro's interest in classical schooling was not entirely piqued. He often discovered that he was more attracted to the world outside of the classroom, where he could see and engage with New York City's eclectic cast of personalities.

De Niro's love for acting started to take form when he was a teenager. At the age of 10, he appeared on stage for the first time in a school production of "The Wizard of Oz," as the Cowardly Lion. He developed a passion for acting after this encounter, seeing its potential as a narrative and expressive medium. Inspired by this early success, De Niro decided to take acting more seriously.

He enrolled in Lee Strasberg's Actors Studio and subsequently the Stella Adler Conservatory, where he studied method acting.

Key players in De Niro's growth as an actor were Stella Adler and Lee Strasberg. De Niro gained a strong foundation in the profession from Strasberg's exacting method acting approaches and Adler's focus on emotional sincerity and inventiveness. These early experiences gave him a strong sense of authenticity and the need to thoroughly embrace his characters—values that would come to characterize his career.

Early on in his acting career, De Niro showed a tremendous dedication to become an expert in his field. He would hone his craft for hours on end, studying the methods of master actors and challenging himself to go into the depths of human feeling. This time of hard training and introspection had

Breaking Barriers, Defying Expectations, and Inspiring Generations

a pivotal role in molding him into the actor he would become.

De Niro's dedication to acting solidified when he entered maturity after growing up. He started taking on bigger parts in independent and off-Broadway companies, further establishing his skill and commitment. De Niro never wavered in his determination in the face of industry instability and competition. His unwavering confidence in his skills and his unrelenting quest of perfection propelled him.

In summation, a combination of personal struggles, creative absorption, and a growing love for acting characterized Robert De Niro's early years in New York City. The thriving cultural milieu of Greenwich Village, in conjunction with the counsel of prominent mentors and his inherent perseverance, established the foundation for his subsequent achievements. These early encounters not only influenced his acting

Breaking Barriers, Defying Expectations, and Inspiring Generations

style but also gave him the tenacity and commitment that would later define his illustrious career. As this book progresses, we'll discover how these early influences shaped and motivated De Niro to go against the grain, shatter stereotypes, and inspire a generation.

Finding Your Acting Passion

A teenage Robert De Niro was finding the roots of a desire that would later grow into a renowned career in the busy neighborhoods of New York City.

De Niro had a very creative upbringing. His father was an abstract expressionist painter and his mother was a poet and painter, thus they created a supportive atmosphere for creative endeavors. But young Robert's mind was really captured by the world of acting.

When De Niro enrolled at the High School of Music & Art in New York, he was surrounded by classmates who were as passionate about the arts as he was. But he found the conventional school environment oppressive, so at sixteen, he left to focus on acting full-time. Although this choice was unorthodox and dangerous, it demonstrated

Breaking Barriers, Defying Expectations, and Inspiring Generations

De Niro's early resolve and steadfast devotion to his cause.

De Niro's early years in the acting profession were characterized by intense training and a focus on method acting. Stella Adler, a well-known acting instructor, had a major influence on him because of her focus on psychological reality and emotional honesty. Supporter of the Stanislavski method, Adler urged her pupils to use their own experiences and feelings to give their characters authenticity. She helped De Niro develop his capacity to get deeply into his characters, which would later become a defining characteristic of his work.

At the Actors Studio, De Niro received training from Lee Strasberg in addition to Adler. The methods De Niro was creating were further supported by Strasberg's method acting approach. De Niro spent a lot of time at the Actors Studio working on scenes and delving into the motivations and

Breaking Barriers, Defying Expectations, and Inspiring Generations

psychology of the characters. His approach to acting was greatly influenced by this intense study phase, which helped him to embody the parts for which he would later become well-known.

In these early years, De Niro worked on short films and off-Broadway shows, playing a range of characters. He gained a solid practical basis and a greater comprehension of the needs of his chosen career from these experiences, which were priceless. Every part, no matter how minor, was a chance for him to hone his skill and try out new acting techniques. This unwavering dedication to perfection and ongoing self-development prepared him for his success in the future.

De Niro's performance in Brian De Palma's 1968 satire picture "Greetings," which examined the Vietnam War conscription, was a turning point in his early career and demonstrated his aptitude and adaptability. Both reviewers and directors were impressed by his performance, which established him as a talented actor with enormous promise. After this part, De Niro worked with De Palma once again on "Hi, Mom!" (1970), which solidified his status as a rising star in the business.

De Niro's dedication to his profession remained unwavering as he advanced in his career. He attacked every new endeavor with the same fervor and commitment that characterized his formative years. He stood out from his classmates because he was eager to take chances and give his all in his responsibilities. Early experiences for De Niro, including his training under Adler and Strasberg and his first movie parts, set him up for an incredible career.

Looking back on these early years, it's evident that De Niro's love of acting was a deep calling rather than just a passing fad. Unwavering passion for his work marked his path from a young lad in Greenwich Village to a budding actor. This period in De Niro's life serves as a tribute to the value of tenacity, intense training, and a readiness to fully embrace one's passion.

The knowledge gained from Robert De Niro's formative years offers priceless insights into the creation of a cinematic icon, as we continue to examine his extraordinary career. Aspiring actors and everyone else attempting to follow their passion with uncompromising devotion and honesty might find inspiration in his narrative.

This chapter offers a thorough and expert summary of Robert De Niro's early acting love, emphasizing the major events and forces that influenced his path.

Mentors and Family as Influences

Robert De Niro's early life experiences had a big impact on his path to become one of the most celebrated performers of his time. These formative experiences—which included mentorship from influential individuals and his creative family background—were crucial in helping him refine his technique and pave the way for success.

Robert De Niro Jr. was born August 17, 1943, in New York City, and raised in a creative household. Both of his parents, Virginia Admiral and Robert De Niro Sr., were successful painters. Virginia was a gifted painter and poet, and De Niro Sr. was a well-known abstract expressionist painter. Young Robert was introduced to the world of art and creativity at a young age since their house was a sanctuary for creative expression. His enjoyment of the arts and his final professional choice were definitely shaped by this supportive atmosphere.

Even though De Niro's parents divorced when he was only two years old, he remained close to both of them and they both gave him insightful advice and insights into life. Virginia, his tough, self-reliant mother, gave him a strong sense of fortitude and willpower. She pushed him to follow his passion despite the uncertainty associated with a career in the arts and supported his early interest in performing. Her steadfast faith in his ability gave him a strong base on which to grow in confidence.

Even though he was often preoccupied with his own creative pursuits, Robert De Niro Sr. also had a lasting impression on his son. Young Robert saw great resonance in De Niro Sr.'s devotion to his trade, his quest for creative recognition, and his determination to uphold artistic integrity. He learned about the sacrifices and tenacity needed to thrive in a creative area by seeing his father traverse the difficulties of the art business.

De Niro's early schooling, in addition to his parents, had a big impact on how his acting career developed. He had professional acting instruction while attending the esteemed Fiorello H. LaGuardia High School of Music & Art and Performing Arts. It was at this point that he realized the discipline and rigor required by performing. This was a critical time in his career since it equipped him with the fundamental information and technical abilities that would later support his performances.

Nonetheless, De Niro discovered some of his most significant mentors outside of the classroom. Stella Adler, a renowned acting instructor and Group Theatre member, had a crucial role in his growth as an actor. De Niro connected with Adler's method of acting because it placed a strong emphasis on the value of emotional honesty and creativity. Her lessons promoted a genuine connection to the subject and a thorough investigation of character, going beyond simple technique. De Niro gained the energy and commitment to every part that would become his signature under Adler's tutelage.

The co-founder of the Actors Studio, Lee Strasberg, was another important influence in De Niro's life. De Niro's approach to acting was influenced by Strasberg's method acting approaches, which emphasized using personal experiences to shape performances. De Niro really accepted the ideas of authenticity and emotional honesty, which were central to Strasberg's philosophy. He developed a deeper understanding of his characters under Strasberg's tutelage, which allowed him to perform with a degree of realism and nuance that distinguished him from his contemporaries.

De Niro gained a strong foundation and a clear awareness of the challenges of his chosen career from these early inspirations and mentors. His upbringing in the arts, his formal education, and the guidance of prominent figures in the field gave him the skills and perspective required to meet the demands of an acting profession. They also ingrained in him a never-ending dedication to his trade and a tireless work ethic.

These guiding forces continued to assist De Niro as he set out on his career path. They influenced his willingness to take chances, his commitment to sincerity, and his acting style. His performances had a depth and complexity that would come to define him, and this was partly due to the lessons he had received from his teachers and family.

To sum up, Robert De Niro's early mentors and inspirations had a significant impact on his career. His parents' creative atmosphere, together with the direction of well-known

Breaking Barriers, Defying Expectations, and Inspiring Generations

acting instructors like Stella Adler and Lee Strasberg, gave him a special combination of imagination, dexterity, and nuance. His remarkable path was made possible by these foundational experiences, which allowed him to shatter stereotypes, confound expectations, and motivate audiences and performers of all ages. We will see as we dive further into his biography how these early inspirations remained relevant throughout his remarkable career, molding the icon that is Robert De Niro.

Hollywood Breakthrough

Being a Hollywood superstar is not always an easy feat, and Robert De Niro's road was no different. Even though he had skill from an early age, it took tenacity and a number of calculated decisions to turn that talent into important parts in the very competitive Hollywood industry.

During his adolescent years, De Niro's love for acting was sparked by his early experiences in theater and modest cinema parts, which highlighted his unique raw ability. Following his training at the American Workshop and the Stella Adler Conservatory, De Niro gained a solid foundation in method acting, which would go on to become his signature style. In addition to helping him polish his skills, these early schooling experiences gave him a deep appreciation for acting, which motivated him for the rest of his career.

Breaking Barriers, Defying Expectations, and Inspiring Generations

In the 1968 Brian De Palma picture "*Greetings*," one of De Niro's first notable parts was played. A far cry from the popular fare of the day, this quirky comedy about three young men seeking to dodge the conscription for the Vietnam War gave De Niro a great chance to demonstrate his versatility. Another De Palma production that came after "*Greetings*" was "Hi, Mom!" (1970), in which Robert De Niro played Jon Rubin once again. Even though they weren't huge blockbusters at the box office, these movies received positive reviews and showed off De Niro's versatility in playing unique, complicated roles.

For De Niro, the early 1970s were a time of great development and activity. While his roles in the 1971 films "*The Gang That Couldn't Shoot Straight*" and "*Born to Win*" helped him to expand his CV, it wasn't until 1973's "*Bang the Drum Slowly*" that he started to get worldwide recognition. De

Breaking Barriers, Defying Expectations, and Inspiring Generations

Niro portrayed slow-witted catcher Bruce Pearson in this moving baseball tale, who was given a grave diagnosis. He received critical praise for his poignant and profoundly touching performance, which also announced to Hollywood the arrival of a significant new talent.

But the real turning point in De Niro's career came when he worked with filmmaker Martin Scorsese on the 1973 movie "*Mean Streets*". In the role of Johnny Boy, an imprudent small-time criminal, De Niro gave a very intense performance. In addition to being a critical triumph, "*Mean Streets*" forged the strong artistic alliance between De Niro and Scorsese, who would go on to make some of the most iconic movies in history.

De Niro's breakthrough performance in "*Mean Streets*" brought him to the attention of the public and helped secure his place as the main man in Hollywood, Vito Corleone in "*The Godfather Part II*" (1974). Under Francis Ford Coppola's direction, De Niro brought a youthful Vito Corleone to life in a performance that was both distinctively his and reverent to Marlon Brando's depiction in the first "*The Godfather*" film. In order to prepare for the part, De Niro studied the dialect of Sicily and immersed himself in early 20th-century New York society. His reputation as one of the most committed and gifted performers of his time was cemented when he won the Academy Award for Best Supporting Actor.

De Niro's reckless approach to a variety of jobs and his dedication to authenticity define his early career. He did not stop at playing roles; he became them, changing both emotionally and physically to give them an unmatched depth and reality. During this time in his career, he demonstrated his remarkable variety as an actor and set the stage for the legendary parts that would come after.

Breaking Barriers, Defying Expectations, and Inspiring Generations

Although Robert De Niro's rise from struggling actor to Hollywood fame wasn't swift nor simple, his early performances show his unrelenting commitment to his art. Every show served as a stepping stone, helping him develop the abilities, standing, and self-assurance that would catapult him into the realm of cinematic mythology. These early years bear witness to the value of tenacity, risk-taking instincts, and an unwavering pursuit of excellence—elements that have shaped De Niro's remarkable career and continue to motivate a new generation of performers.

It is crucial to recognize the importance of these early roles as we continue to examine De Niro's life and career. They not only signaled the start of an amazing voyage, but they also laid the foundation for a legacy that would shatter stereotypes, challenge expectations, and motivate a great number of people globally.

Chapter 2

Mean Streets and Scorsese

The history of film is full of legendary alliances that have influenced the industry; one of the most well-known is the long-lasting cooperation between actor Robert De Niro and director Martin Scorsese. This chapter explores the origins of their renowned collaboration, showing how "Mean Streets" not only signaled the start of their working relationship but also laid the groundwork for a string of ground-breaking movies that would revolutionize American cinema.

Both De Niro and Scorsese were rising stars hoping to leave their mark in the early 1970s. With a sharp eye for gritty realism

Breaking Barriers, Defying Expectations, and Inspiring Generations

and an unmatched ability to capture the raw energy of urban life, filmmaker Martin Scorsese was searching for an actor who could give his characters a sense of authenticity and nuance. Here comes Robert De Niro, an actor who was a perfect fit for Scorsese's vision because of his meticulous approach and unwavering dedication to his work.

The movie "*Mean Streets*," which would later come to symbolize the urban experience of the period and usher in a new age in filmmaking, brought their paths together. The film, which is set in Little Italy in New York, explores the intricacies of morality, friendship, and loyalty while providing a realistic and unvarnished portrait of life in the underworld of the city. The portrayal of Johnny Boy by De Niro, a carefree and erratic young guy, was astounding. His portrayal of the character's charm and danger demonstrated his

Breaking Barriers, Defying Expectations, and Inspiring Generations

extraordinary versatility and made him stand out as a formidable actor.

"Mean Streets" garnered critical acclaim for its authentic portrayal of city life and the evident rapport between De Niro and Harvey Keitel. But it was De Niro's interpretation of Johnny Boy that grabbed the interest of critics and viewers alike. His portrayal of Johnny Boy's frenetic energy and unpredictable nature was a masterclass in character immersion, cementing Johnny Boy's legacy as a significant figure in cinematic history.

The movie signaled the start of a collaboration based on respect for one another and a common love of narrative. A creative chemistry that would inspire them to push the limits of their profession was found between Scorsese and De Niro. Their cooperation sprang from a strong grasp of the roles they aimed to play and a resolute dedication to realism.

Breaking Barriers, Defying Expectations, and Inspiring Generations

With the box office triumph of "*Mean Streets*," De Niro and Scorsese proceeded to go further into the darkest facets of the human condition with a string of iconic movies. Their collaboration was further solidified when "Taxi Driver," one of the most significant films in cinematic history, was released in 1976. It was both eerie and engrossing to see De Niro play mentally disturbed Vietnam War veteran Travis Bickle. His well-known comment, "You talkin' to me?" cemented itself in popular culture, showcasing his capacity to create emotionally charged moments for viewers.

With the release of "Raging Bull" in 1980, which highlighted De Niro's tremendous commitment to his profession, the partnership reached new heights. In order to faithfully capture the many phases of boxer Jake LaMotta's life, actor Robert De Niro underwent a drastic physical makeover, gaining and shedding a considerable amount of weight. He won the Academy Award for Best Actor for his dedication to sincerity, and the movie is often considered as one of the best in movie history.

Their collaboration flourished with a series of critically acclaimed movies, such as "*The King of Comedy*," "*Goodfellas*," "*Cape Fear*," and "*Casino*." All of these projects demonstrated their ability to explore intricate character and story development, resulting in films that were both critically and commercially successful. They continuously questioned the rules of conventional narrative via their art, giving viewers an unvarnished look at the human condition.

Beyond the awards and praise from critics, De Niro and Scorsese's partnership is proof of the potency of creative synergy. Their collaboration is a perfect example of how a director and actor may collaborate to accomplish remarkable creative results when they have a strong understanding and regard for one another. Together, they have inspired a generation of actors and filmmakers to follow their profession with integrity and enthusiasm in addition to providing viewers with entertainment.

To sum up, the collaboration between Martin Scorsese and Robert De Niro, which started with "*Mean Streets*," is among the most recognizable in cinematic history. Their partnership has resulted in some of the most enduring and significant movies of the last fifty years, each of which is proof of their unwavering dedication to quality and common vision. As we go further into De Niro's career, his collaborations with Scorsese continue to be a pillar of his legacy, demonstrating the deep effect of their artistic collaboration on the film industry.

Making an Icon as a Taxi Driver

Few movies have had as much of an impact on cinematic history as Martin Scorsese's "Taxi Driver." The 1976 release of the movie cemented Robert De Niro's place in the top cast of films and cemented his depiction of Travis Bickle into popular culture. "Taxi Driver" is not just a movie; it's a cinematic classic that explores a damaged man's mind in great detail, and Robert De Niro's performance is what makes it so powerful.

The Partnership with Scorsese

Robert De Niro and Martin Scorsese had developed a solid professional rapport by the time "Taxi Driver" was being produced. Their earlier work together on "Mean

Streets" had established the foundation for a cooperation that would challenge cinematic conventions. Recognizing that De Niro could fully inhabit any role, director Scorsese gave him the part of Vietnam War veteran Travis Bickle, a mentally disturbed man traversing the seedy streets of New York City.

De Niro's Intense Get Ready

Legendary is De Niro's dedication to the character of Travis Bickle. De Niro, who is renowned for his method acting style, went above and beyond to fully embody the role. He infamously got a license to drive cabs in New York City, spending weeks fully immersed in the nightlife that Bickle would have known. Thanks to his extensive preparation, De Niro was able to portray the subtleties of a man on the verge of insanity, giving his portrayal an unmatched level of realism.

Breaking Barriers, Defying Expectations, and Inspiring Generations

Apart from his physical training, De Niro also studied Bickle's psychology in great detail. He collaborated extensively with Paul Schrader, the author, and Martin Scorsese to comprehend Bickle's aspirations, anxieties, and motives. Because of this careful preparation, the character was portrayed in a way that was both eerie and sympathetic, letting viewers see humanity despite her extreme flaws.

The Scene of Transformation

The mirror scene, which is partly improvised by Robert De Niro, is one of the most memorable scenes in "Taxi Driver." It depicts Travis Bickle rehearsing his encounter with made-up opponents and saying the now-famous phrase, "You talkin' to me?" Acting prowess is shown by De Niro's ability to capture Bickle's boiling wrath and shattered mental condition. Since then, the moment has grown to be among the most often cited and discussed in movie

Breaking Barriers, Defying Expectations, and Inspiring Generations

history, solidifying De Niro's reputation as a movie legend.

Influence on Culture and Criteria

"Taxi Driver" received the coveted Palme d'Or at its 1976 Cannes Film Festival debut. Both reviewers and viewers were moved by the film's realistic depiction of urban deterioration and its examination of violence and loneliness. De Niro received much praise for his portrayal and was nominated for a Best Actor Academy Award. His depiction of Travis Bickle became a standard for conversations about alienation from society, mental health, and the effects of war on veterans.

"Taxi Driver" was an instant hit, but it had a long-lasting impact on popular culture and film. Numerous actors and directors have been influenced by it, and De Niro's portrayal is often held up as a model for character-driven narrative. The film's themes of disappointment and isolation are still relevant and resonate with audiences of a new age.

Retrospection and Legacy

In retrospect, De Niro's performance in "Taxi Driver" marks a turning point in his career. It demonstrated his capacity to fully inhabit a part, a talent that would come to characterize many of his later performances. For Scorsese, the movie signaled the start of a successful partnership that would produce many important motion picture moments.

In interviews, De Niro has discussed playing Travis Bickle with a combination of humility and pride. He recognizes that the success of the movie was a team effort, attributing significant factors to Schrader's screenplay and Scorsese's vision. Nonetheless, De Niro's portrayal—which is both menacing and moving—remains the focal point of "Taxi Driver," captivating viewers time and time again.

In summary

In Robert De Niro's remarkable career, "Taxi Driver" is more than simply a movie; it's a pivotal piece that highlights his commitment to his work. His performance as Travis Bickle is a masterpiece in method acting, one that not only won praise from critics but also had a lasting impact on popular culture. By becoming a legend, De Niro established a high standard for future generations of performers and proved the transformational power of film.

This chapter encapsulates the spirit of Robert De Niro's legendary performance in "Taxi Driver," highlighting his commitment, the teamwork involved in making the movie, and its lasting influence.

Breaking Barriers, Defying Expectations, and Inspiring Generations

Changing to Fit a Part

Few performances in Robert De Niro's illustrious career stand out as strikingly as his portrayal of Jake LaMotta in "Raging Bull." The film, directed by Martin Scorsese, is frequently hailed as one of the greatest in American history, and a major factor in its ongoing acclaim is De Niro's dedication to the role. This chapter dives into the production of "Raging Bull," examining De Niro's remarkable change for the part and the significant influence it had on both his acting career and skill.

A biographical sports drama called "Raging Bull" follows middleweight boxer Jake LaMotta's turbulent existence. LaMotta's ascent in the boxing world and his eventual decline, characterized by angry outbursts, strained relationships, and inner despair, are shown in the movie. In the realm of method acting, De Niro endured a physical and psychological metamorphosis that has since become famous in order to successfully play LaMotta.

De Niro put in a very thorough amount of practice for "Raging Bull". Distinguished by his deep focus on character development, he elevated method acting to unprecedented levels. He started by reading LaMotta's autobiography, viewing hours of bout film, and doing a thorough analysis of his life. Not only did De Niro want to emulate the physical attributes of LaMotta, but he also wanted to absorb his inner anguish and psychological composition.

In order to play LaMotta as he really was, De Niro undertook a rigorous physical training program. He received instruction from LaMotta himself, picking up the subtleties of boxing and perfecting the moves that made LaMotta a dangerous foe in the ring. For months, De Niro worked on his physical fitness, jogged, and sparred to become a credible boxer. His hard work paid off as he was able to convey the unadulterated, feral fury that typified LaMotta's fighting style.

But what really made De Niro's performance stand out was his willingness to go through a drastic bodily makeover. LaMotta is shown as being overweight and unfit in the latter portions of the movie, which is a sharp contrast to his previous, athletic persona. In order to do this, De Niro put on an incredible sixty pounds. Gaining weight was more than simply a way to change his look; it was also a way to represent LaMotta's fall into self-destruction and the psychological and physical toll it had on him.

There were dangers associated with deciding to put on that much weight. De Niro's condition was constantly watched, and the procedure needed to be carefully planned and carried out. He went to Italy and quickly gained weight by indulging in a high-calorie diet. Production was momentarily stopped due to the drastic change, which allowed De Niro the time he needed to put on the weight and resume shooting.

Beyond only cosmetic adjustments, De Niro gave the character his all attention. He dug far into LaMotta's mind, trying to make sense of the intricacies of a man consumed by anger and insecurity. De Niro was able to provide a performance that was both physically and emotionally credible because of this psychological absorption. His performance perfectly encapsulated the paradoxes of LaMotta's persona—a guy who was a fierce competitor outside of the ring and a terribly disturbed person within.

De Niro's transformational performance and thorough preparation produced an astounding outcome. The movie "Raging

Bull" received positive reviews from critics, and De Niro's performance as LaMotta was well-received. His ability to capture the character's emotional depth and visceral intensity enthralled both critics and viewers. De Niro's status as one of the best performers of his time was cemented when he won his second Academy Award for Best Actor for the performance.

"Raging Bull" had a significant influence on acting technique as well. Numerous performers were motivated to push the limits of their own performances by De Niro's dedication to changing himself for the part, which established a new benchmark for method acting. His determination to put himself through psychological and physical pain in order to maintain authenticity set a standard of commitment that has since been adopted by the business.

"Raging Bull" is still a monument to the creative wizardry of De Niro and Scorsese's collaboration, despite its success and impact. Their collaboration, characterized by mutual respect and artistic synergy, made it possible for them to produce a picture that went beyond the biography genre and gave an honest and unvarnished view of the human condition.

To sum up, Robert De Niro's change for "Raging Bull" is a pivotal point in his career and a significant development in the history of film. His performance as Jake LaMotta demonstrates his unmatched commitment to his profession and is a masterclass in method acting. In addition to giving a complicated character life in this part, De Niro redefined honesty in cinema and paved the way for a new generation of performers.

Breaking Barriers, Defying Expectations, and Inspiring Generations

The Acting Methods of Robert De Niro

Robert De Niro is a great actor whose success is largely due to his intense devotion to Method acting. De Niro's approach to his profession has been greatly influenced by this method, which was established by Lee Strasberg and has its roots in the teachings of Constantin Stanislavski. This chapter enters into the intricacies of Method acting and the ways in which De Niro's use of this approach has distinguished him in the film industry.

In order to provide realistic performances, method acting encourages performers to connect deeply and fully with the role by drawing from their own feelings and experiences. For De Niro, this entails a complete psychological and physical metamorphosis into the role he is playing, not merely learning lines and hitting marks.

Breaking Barriers, Defying Expectations, and Inspiring Generations

This dedication is shown by the fact that he has gone above and above to thoroughly embody some of his most well-known roles.

De Niro's training for the part of Jake LaMotta in "Raging Bull" (1980) is among the most stunning illustrations of his commitment to Method acting. Martin Scorsese was the film's director, and De Niro had to play LaMotta as a broken-down guy in his latter years as well as a fighter in his peak. In order to do this, De Niro underwent intense training in boxing, working closely with LaMotta to fully understand the subtleties of the sport, and also put on a substantial amount of weight in order to accurately portray LaMotta's physical deterioration. This metamorphosis was more than just a physical change; it was an attempt to capture the spirit of the character at various points in his life, which made the representation very realistic and poignant.

Breaking Barriers, Defying Expectations, and Inspiring Generations

De Niro's commitment to Method acting is further shown by his training for the part of Travis Bickle in "Taxi Driver" (1976). De Niro got an actual taxi driver's license and spent weeks operating a cab in New York City in order to truly portray a psychologically ill Vietnam War veteran turned cab driver. De Niro's understanding of Bickle's loneliness and alienation from society was made possible by his total absorption into the character's reality, and this understanding gave his portrayal a raw, frightening realism that viewers have never forgotten.

De Niro had to act in both English and Sicilian Italian for his role as a young Vito Corleone in "The Godfather Part II" (1974). In order to guarantee his authenticity and fluency in the part, De Niro underwent intensive language instruction. The figure initially portrayed by Marlon Brando gained depth and coherence from his ability to credibly represent the youthful father of the

Corleone family. De Niro's portrayal was so strong that it won him the Academy Award for Best Supporting Actor, demonstrating his extraordinary talent for vividly imagining complicated people via painstaking research and total absorption.

De Niro often goes above and beyond the stage makeup for his performances. He's similarly well-prepared psychologically. In an effort to comprehend the deepest sensations and ideas of his characters, he painstakingly investigates their histories, motives, and psychological composition. Examining the character's past, their connections, and the society they live in are all part of this process. By doing this, De Niro is able to provide performances that are true to life and nuanced, endowing his characters with a lasting impression and relatability.

His portrayal of the ominous Max Cady in "Cape Fear" (1991) demonstrates this dedication to reality. In addition to going through a physical makeover—gaining muscle and getting fake tattoos all over his body—he also extensively collaborated with a speech coach to improve Cady's Southern accent for this part. In order to comprehend the thoughts of a spiteful ex-convict, he also sought advice from a psychotherapist. The result of their efforts was a terrifying representation that enthralled and scared spectators.

De Niro also approaches acting with a great regard for teamwork. He often collaborates extensively with directors, writers, and other performers to fully grasp his role in the larger narrative. This collaborative attitude improves the movie's overall quality since De Niro's suggestions and analysis serve to strengthen the story and character development.

Beyond his well-known metamorphoses, De Niro's acting style has had a more subdued impact on his roles. De Niro's strong emotional bond with his characters is evident in movies like "The Deer Hunter" (1978) and "Awakenings" (1990). His ability to create characters that are both real and appealing via nuanced representations of complicated emotions is a testament to the strength of Method acting.

Robert De Niro's reputation as one of the best performers of his time has been cemented by his commitment to Method acting. His readiness to fully commit to his parts, go through emotional and physical changes, and work closely with his colleagues has produced some of the most iconic performances in the history of film. De Niro continues to shatter limits, exceed expectations, and inspire viewers and performers alike with his relentless dedication to his work.

Chapter 3

A Performance That Defines a Career

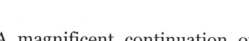

A magnificent continuation of a tale that goes into themes of treachery, family, and power, "The Godfather Part II" remains as a towering masterpiece in the pantheon of great American movies. This movie marked a turning point in Robert De Niro's developing career, not simply another part. As the youthful Vito Corleone, a role already made legendary by Marlon Brando in the first "The Godfather," De Niro had to live up to a great deal of pressure. In addition to having to be flawless, his portrayal had to do tribute to the legacy of one of the most recognizable characters in movie history.

De Niro's casting in "The Godfather Part II" was evidence of his developing skill as an

Breaking Barriers, Defying Expectations, and Inspiring Generations

actor. Francis Ford Coppola, the director, was aware of De Niro's exceptional skill and thought he might give Vito Corleone a fresh perspective. An actor who could convey the subtleties of a young immigrant's ascent to prominence—a figure who is both merciless and very human—was required for this part. De Niro was the perfect option because of his careful approach to acting, commitment to realism, and ability to capture the nuance of difficult characters.

The way that De Niro trained for the Vito Corleone part is almost legendary. Well-known for his dedication to method acting, he fully submerged himself in the role. To make sure his interpretation was true to the role, De Niro studied the Sicilian dialect for months. In order to understand the surroundings and culture that influenced Vito Corleone's early years, he even went to Sicily. His portrayal reflected his commitment to comprehending the character's past and intentions, which gave

Breaking Barriers, Defying Expectations, and Inspiring Generations

it a deeper quality that both fans and critics found appealing.

Marlon Brando, whose depiction of Vito Corleone in "The Godfather" was already legendary, was one of the trickiest parts of De Niro's performance. De Niro tackled this task with a creative and respectful attitude. He tried to make the role his own while retaining its core, as opposed to copying Brando. His interpretation emphasized Vito's transformation from a young guy to a strong father, echoing Brando's portrayal with nuanced bodily cues and a calm passion.

Acting at its best, De Niro's depiction of Vito Corleone in "The Godfather Part II" His proficiency was shown by his ability to capture the character's inner conflict and desire with little words and strong facial expressions. With a masterful balance between measured restraint and raw passion, the sequences showing Vito's

Breaking Barriers, Defying Expectations, and Inspiring Generations

ascent to power—including the famous scene in which he exacts retribution on the local mafia boss—were presented in a way that made a lasting impression.

The economic and critical triumph of "The Godfather Part II" cemented Robert De Niro's place among the greatest performers of his period. De Niro won the Oscar for Best Supporting Actor, while the movie took home six Academy Awards, including Best Picture. This acknowledgement was a turning point in his career, confirming his ability and creating a wealth of fresh prospects.

De Niro's portrayal in "The Godfather Part II" further showed his capacity to work well with creative filmmakers. His collaboration with Francis Ford Coppola was characterized by a common dedication to narrative and a mutual respect. This partnership paved the path for De Niro's next endeavors, in which he would

Breaking Barriers, Defying Expectations, and Inspiring Generations

consistently push the limits of his ability and strive to give his characters a sense of realism and nuance.

In addition to the recognition and prizes, De Niro's depiction of Vito Corleone had a lasting impact on the motion picture business. It illustrated the value of thorough planning and the need of respecting the heritage of a character while bringing something new to it. De Niro's approach to this part is an example for young actors, highlighting the value of commitment, study, and a thorough comprehension of the character's psychology.

A performance that not only summed up Robert De Niro's early Hollywood years but also set the bar high for his subsequent work, "The Godfather Part II" continues to be a seminal effort in his career. His depiction of the youthful Vito Corleone is evidence of his unwavering character, his devotion to perfection, and his capacity to go above and beyond. Recalling this crucial part brings to mind De Niro's lasting influence on the film industry as well as his status as one of the finest performers of all time.

A Dynamic Pair

Few collaborations in movie history can compare to the dynamic team of Robert De Niro and Martin Scorsese. They have worked together for decades, creating some of the most recognizable and well-received movies in movie history. Filmmakers and actors alike continue to be inspired and influenced by the legacy that Scorsese's visionary direction and Robert De Niro's revolutionary acting created.

The collaboration started in 1973 with "Mean Streets," a grim, unapologetic portrayal of life in Little Italy, New York. Johnny Boy, a brash and charming small-time criminal, was De Niro's portrayal that first distinguished him as an actor with extraordinary depth and passion. De Niro's riveting performance and Scorsese's unvarnished portrayal of urban life heralded the start of a creative partnership that would revolutionize modern cinema.

The movie "Taxi Driver" from 1976 is perhaps the most famous product of their partnership. One of the most acclaimed roles in movie history is De Niro's portrayal of Travis Bickle, a mentally disturbed Vietnam War veteran who works as a cab driver in New York City. Both his famous remark, "You talkin' to me?" and his terrifying depiction of Bickle's spiral into insanity has become part of popular culture. With its inventive use of lighting, camera angles, and Bernard Herrmann's eerie soundtrack, director Scorsese produced a visceral experience that moviegoers will never forget.

The pair's next significant project together, "Raging Bull" (1980), cemented De Niro and

Breaking Barriers, Defying Expectations, and Inspiring Generations

Scorsese's status as legends in the film industry. Many people consider De Niro's portrayal of violent and troubled boxer Jake LaMotta to be one of the best roles in movie history. In order to faithfully portray LaMotta's physical metamorphosis, De Niro reportedly put on sixty pounds, demonstrating his unmatched devotion to his work. The violence and sadness of LaMotta's life were conveyed by Scorsese's harsh black-and-white photography and uncompromising directing, which won the movie several accolades, including an Academy Award for Best Actor for Robert De Niro.

In "The King of Comedy" (1982), De Niro portrayed the naive wannabe comic Rupert Pupkin, which changed the course of their partnership. The damaging effects of fame and obsession were brought to light by the film's dark humor and De Niro's unnerving performance. Though originally received with negative reviews, the picture has subsequently garnered a cult following and is now recognized as one of Scorsese's most daring works.

"Goodfellas" (1990) is another cornerstone of the De Niro-Scorsese team. De Niro's depiction of Jimmy Conway, a seasoned gangster, provided a subtle richness to the character. The film's fast-paced plot, dynamic editing, and riveting performances from the whole ensemble produced a cinematic classic that has inspired other films in the criminal genre. Scorsese's painstaking attention to detail and his ability to extract strong performances from his actors demonstrated the strength of their relationship.

In 1995, De Niro and Scorsese reunited for "Casino," a grandiose epic about the rise and collapse of a Las Vegas gambling empire. De Niro's depiction of Sam "Ace" Rothstein, a methodical and calculating casino operator, was both intriguing and heartbreaking. With its ornate set pieces and captivating storyline, Scorsese's director created a striking image of corruption and avarice. The movie's critical and financial success served as further evidence of their collaboration's lasting influence.

With "The Irishman" (2019), a complex crime drama that brought De Niro, Scorsese, and his regular collaborators Al Pacino and Joe Pesci back together, their partnership extended into the twenty-first century. De Niro was a masterpiece in nuance and reflection in his depiction of mafia hitman Frank Sheeran, who was contemplating his life. By skillfully using digital de-aging technology, the movie demonstrated De Niro's adaptability and endurance as an actor by allowing him to represent Sheeran throughout many decades. With its deliberate tempo and thoughtful tone, Scorsese's directing offered De Niro's nuanced performance a suitable canvas.

Breaking Barriers, Defying Expectations, and Inspiring Generations

The corpus of work that De Niro and Scorsese have created is timeless and transcends genre. Their mutual dedication to realism, narrative, and pushing the limits of the film industry has produced movies that elicit strong feelings and thoughts in addition to being enjoyable. They have created a legacy that inspires and influences others to this day, showcasing the amazing possibilities of artistic cooperation.

It's clear from considering Robert De Niro and Martin Scorsese's extraordinary journey together that their collaboration is proof of the potency of creative synergy. They have left an enduring impression on the film industry by shattering boundaries, defying expectations, and inspiring generations via their works.

Breaking Barriers, Defying Expectations, and Inspiring Generations

Oscar Winning

The Academy Awards are the highest accolade in the film industry, serving as a symbol of an artist's extraordinary ability and commitment to the medium. For Robert De Niro, receiving the Oscar was not just a recognition of his talent but also a confirmation of his unwavering commitment to his work. His story of achieving this esteemed award is one of tenacity, inspirational performances, and a steadfast dedication to genuineness.

The Godfather Part II, directed by Francis Ford Coppola, was a follow-up to the critically acclaimed "The Godfather." Robert De Niro won his first Oscar in 1975 for his performance as Vito Corleone. His portrayal of the young Vito Corleone was nothing short of a masterclass in acting, capturing the character's complexity and depth with remarkable precision. In addition to having a thorough comprehension of the role, he had to be able to portray a variety of emotions using his delicate facial expressions and sophisticated movements.

De Niro immersed himself in the life and culture of the character he was to play in order to be ready for the part. In order to give Vito Corleone the most genuine representation possible, he studied Sicilian dialects for months. One of De Niro's defining characteristics as an actor was his commitment to honesty, which came through in his performance. His depiction was warmly received by both critics and viewers, and as a result, he was awarded the Academy Award for Best Supporting Actor. His efforts were well worth it.

For De Niro, winning the Oscar for "The Godfather Part II" marked a noteworthy turning point in his career. It made him a

Breaking Barriers, Defying Expectations, and Inspiring Generations

formidable talent in Hollywood and paved the way for him to work with actors and directors of the highest caliber in the future. The prize was a testimonial to his ability to infuse life into complicated characters, a technique that would become his trademark in the years to come.

In 1981, De Niro won his second Oscar for his portrayal as Martin Scorsese's Jake LaMotta in "Raging Bull." This performance, which is widely regarded as one of the best in movie history, demonstrated De Niro's amazing versatility and dedication to his craft. In order to portray a real-life boxer, De Niro had to undergo a rigorous and extreme physical makeover. To accurately depict LaMotta's life phases, from a fit young boxer to an overweight, retired fighter, he underwent substantial weight gain and loss.

Beyond only physical makeovers, "Raging Bull" required extensive planning. To acquire boxing tactics and comprehend the character's psychological complexity, De Niro studied under LaMotta himself. He was able to provide a performance that was unvarnished, primal, and really genuine thanks to this immersive technique. Both audiences and reviewers were enthralled by his depiction of LaMotta's ascent and decline, which was characterized by intense, vulnerable, and contemplative moments.

One of the finest acting performances of his time, De Niro's Oscar for Best Actor for "Raging Bull" was a defining moment in his career. It was an acknowledgment of his steadfast commitment to the acting craft as well as his performance in that movie. The recognition highlighted his capacity to push limits and test himself in every job he played.

De Niro's career and legacy were significantly impacted by her two Oscar victories. It led to a multitude of chances, including working with some of the most well-known directors in the business. In the years that followed these victories, his work kept demonstrating his dedication to quality and love of telling tales. Aspiring performers found inspiration in De Niro's Oscar wins, which showed that genuine talent requires perseverance, devotion, and an unflinching commitment to authenticity.

Beyond the recognition, De Niro's Oscar victories are the result of years of toil, sacrifice, and an unwavering quest for excellence. They serve as evidence of his ability to authentically and deeply inhabit a variety of characters, enthralling viewers and making a lasting impression on the film industry. His story of breaking down boundaries, going against the grain, and inspiring a generation of performers and filmmakers is told in the context of his Oscar triumph.

Breaking Barriers, Defying Expectations, and Inspiring Generations

Thinking back on Robert De Niro's Oscar-winning roles serves as a reminder of the influence of genuine craftsmanship and the strength of commitment. His story is an inspiration to us, motivating us to follow our interests with the same steadfast dedication and to aim for perfection in all we do. His Oscar victories have left a lasting legacy that motivates young people to shatter stereotypes, go against the grain, and make their own impression on the world.

A Bronx Tale, De Niro's Directorial Debut

The move from actor to director is a familiar one in Hollywood history, greeted with doubt and anxiety. However, Robert De Niro felt that this transition into directing was a logical progression of his diverse skill set.

"A Bronx Tale," a 1993 film, is a masterpiece of cinema that perfectly portrays life in the Bronx in the 1960s. The film is a coming-of-age tale that examines issues of family, loyalty, and the attraction of the streets. It is an adaptation of Chazz Palminteri's one-man play of the same name. "A Bronx Tale" depicts a vivid picture of a young child called Calogero, who is caught between the temptation of a local gangster (played by Palminteri) and the advice of his diligent father (played by De

Niro), set against the background of racial tensions and organized crime.

"A Bronx Tale" gave De Niro the chance to explore subjects that were very close to his own background and to demonstrate his directing abilities. De Niro was raised on the streets of New York and was thus well-versed in the local dynamics and cultural quirks that were portrayed in the movie. His attention to detail and unrelenting dedication to authenticity give each frame of "A Bronx Tale" a realistic and profound emotional quality that continues to captivate viewers.

De Niro handled "A Bronx Tale" as a filmmaker with the same attention to detail and commitment that he showed to his playing parts. He collaborated closely with Palminteri to translate the play to the big screen, maintaining the story's core while incorporating his own distinct cinematic viewpoint. De Niro added his own flair to every part of the movie, from casting choices to visual effects, creating a cinematic experience that is at once eminently personal and ageless.

When "A Bronx Tale" was released, it was met with a great deal of praise from critics who praised De Niro's confident directing and the film's accurate depiction of Bronx life. Critics praised it as a remarkable behind-the-camera debut for De Niro, highlighting his aptitude for tying together intricate storylines and drawing strong performances from his ensemble. The movie's box office performance cemented De Niro's standing as a multifaceted and strong artist in the film industry, garnering him recognition as both an actor and a visionary storyteller.

Even after receiving high praise from critics, "A Bronx Tale" has a unique place in the hearts of viewers everywhere. Its ageless themes of redemption, loyalty, and family speak to people of all ages and serve as a moving reminder of the bonds that unite us all. According to De Niro, the movie is a labor of love and a monument to his unwavering enthusiasm for making stories and the ability of movies to shed light on the human condition.

Finally, we conclude by highlighting Robert De Niro's first feature picture, "A Bronx Tale," which is a monument to his creative vision and brilliance. De Niro created a cinematic masterpiece that enthralls viewers and inspires filmmakers worldwide with painstaking attention to detail and a deep comprehension of the subject. We learn more about the creation of "A Bronx Tale," which helps us understand how De Niro developed as an artist and how his influence on the film industry has endured.

Breaking Barriers, Defying Expectations, and Inspiring Generations

Chapter 4

Comedy Exploration

Throughout Robert De Niro's long career, he is most recognized for his powerfully dramatic parts, but there is one interesting exception: his comedic ones. This chapter explores two of De Niro's most well-known comedy roles: "Analyze This" and "Meet the Parents." These roles demonstrate not just the actor's range but also his skill at expressing humor with subtlety and elegance.

Harold Ramis's 1999 film "Analyze This," which stars De Niro and Billy Crystal as comedy heavyweights, tells the amusing story of a neurotic doctor who treats an odd patient—a crime leader who suffers from anxiety attacks. A master of comic timing and nuance, De Niro plays the fierce but fragile gangster Paul Vitti, who seeks treatment. His superb comedic timing and deadpan delivery make him the ideal counterpoint to Crystal's frustrated Dr. Ben Sobel, the psychiatrist. The film's ingenious idea is simply one factor contributing to its popularity; another is De Niro's acceptance of the ridiculousness of the scenario, which draws comedy from the contrast between Vitti's strong demeanor and his inner struggle.

In the 2000 Jay Roach film "Meet the Parents," De Niro plays another humorous part, but one with a distinct flair. Here, De Niro plays Jack Byrnes, a concerned father and former CIA agent who subjects Ben Stiller, who is playing his daughter's suitor, to a series of progressively strange and unpleasant interrogations. De Niro strikes the ideal balance between comedy and sadness in his portrayal of the commanding yet lovably controlling father-in-law-to-be. His ability to portray both aggression and sensitivity gives the character more nuance, which takes the movie from being a lighthearted comedy to a poignant examination of family relationships and the shared dread of rejection.

In these lighthearted parts, De Niro's steadfast devotion to the people and the circumstances they find themselves in sets him unique. Even though he is one of Hollywood's most admired dramatic performers, he treats comedic roles with the same commitment and sincerity, losing himself completely in the ridiculousness of the situations without ever going against his character. De Niro is able to inhabit these humorous characters with the same amount of conviction and seriousness as his more serious performances because of his devotion to authenticity and his innate gift for timing and delivery.

Breaking Barriers, Defying Expectations, and Inspiring Generations

Moreover, De Niro's entry into the comedy genre is evidence of his range as an actor. His versatility and breadth are shown by his ability to move fluidly across genres, even if he may be most recognized for his intensely tragic performances. Few actors can equal De Niro's depth and complexity in his comedy roles, whether he's playing a disturbed gangster seeking treatment or a straight-talking father-in-law who loves lying detector tests.

"Analyze This" and "Meet the Parents" explore themes of vulnerability, family relationships, and the absurdity of ordinary life, giving spectators an insight into the human condition beyond just a good chuckle. De Niro encourages audiences to embrace life's lighter side and find laughter and pleasure in even the most unusual circumstances with his comic performances.

In summary, Robert De Niro's humorous appearances in "Analyze This" and "Meet the Parents" are excellent instances of his ability to maintain the realism and gravity that characterize his serious performances. De Niro demonstrates that laughing is not only the greatest medicine but also a testimonial to the continuing strength of his skill as an actor via his nuanced representations and superb comedic timing.

Getting Ready for Your Role

Authenticity is the secret to producing remarkable and captivating performances in the world of acting. This dedication to genuineness has served as Robert De Niro's compass throughout his distinguished career..

A defining characteristic of De Niro's acting is his commitment to giving his best to the parts he plays. No matter what he's portraying, De Niro goes above and beyond to be really genuine. He goes above and above in his efforts to bring his characters to life on film, from in-depth study to dramatic physical changes.

De Niro's dedication to understanding the psyche and motives of the characters he plays is at the heart of his preparation process. He explores his characters' pasts in great detail in an effort to understand their deepest aspirations, anxieties, and ideas. De Niro is able to give his performances a feeling of emotional depth and complexity that people connect with by means of this process of reflection.

De Niro is renowned for his physical adaptations for roles in addition to his psychological preparation. To guarantee that his representation is as realistic as possible, he goes through extensive training and preparation, which includes everything from weight growth or loss to accent and mannerism mastery. His depiction of boxer Jake LaMotta in "Raging Bull," in which he notably gained over 60 pounds to authentically convey the character's physical deterioration, is a testament to his attention to physicality.

Moreover, De Niro goes above and beyond the movie set in his quest for authenticity. He often immerses himself in the settings of his characters, visiting their hometowns or

Breaking Barriers, Defying Expectations, and Inspiring Generations

interacting with others who have similar experiences or backgrounds. Through complete immersion in his characters' worlds, De Niro learns more about their problems and lives, which enables him to perform with a feeling of realism and honesty.

De Niro has worked with some of the most well-known filmmakers and performers in the business during his career; several of them have complimented him on his commitment to realism. Film directors like Francis Ford Coppola and Martin Scorsese have praised De Niro for his dedication to his work, praising his determination to test the limits of his skills and attention to detail.

From the first phases of study to the last seconds before the cameras shoot. Readers are given access to the actor's approach and thinking process via interviews with De Niro and his colleagues and co-stars, providing a unique window into the head of one of the greatest actors in movie history.

Readers learn about the extent of De Niro's devotion to authenticity and how it has greatly influenced his performances as they work their way through. De Niro's commitment to his work, evident in both his early parts and his most recent endeavors, is a bright example of what can happen when sincerity and enthusiasm meet on screen.

Philanthropy and Entrepreneurial Activities

Robert De Niro's influence goes far beyond acting, as his ventures into business and his dedication to charity bear that. This chapter examines De Niro's business endeavors as well as the noteworthy contributions he has made to a number of charity organizations.

De Niro has shown a strong sense of business throughout his career, using his notoriety and connections to further ventures that are in line with his interests and ambitions. Co-founding the Tribeca Film Festival in 2002 is one of his most renowned endeavors. Since its founding as an initiative to bring Lower Manhattan back to life after the September 11 attacks, the festival has grown to become a prominent venue for independent filmmakers worldwide. The Tribeca Film Festival has developed into a cultural institution under

De Niro's direction, drawing A-list talent and presenting avant-garde films.

Apart from the Tribeca Film Festival, De Niro has made investments in a number of hospitality-related businesses, such as eateries and lodging facilities. His flagship restaurant, Nobu, has won praise from all around the world for its avant-garde fusion food and posh dining atmosphere. Nobu, which has restaurants all over the world, has come to be associated with elegance and refinement, a testament to De Niro's discriminating palate and unwavering pursuit of perfection.

In addition to his business endeavors, De Niro has a strong desire to improve the world and give back to his community. He actively supports issues ranging from environmental protection to arts education via his involvement in many philanthropic organizations. Numerous lives have been impacted by De Niro's charitable work, which has included supporting social fairness, fostering cultural enrichment, and giving opportunity to young people from disadvantaged backgrounds.

Arts education is among the subjects that De Niro is most passionate about. He has devoted his life to ensuring that young people have access to high-quality arts education programs because he really believes in the transformational potential of the arts. Through his support of programs that develop new talent and encourage innovation, De Niro has championed institutions like the Actors Studio and the Tribeca Film Institute.

De Niro is a strong supporter of environmental protection in addition to arts education. He has contributed his voice to several environmental campaigns and efforts because he understands how vital it is to combat climate change. De Niro is dedicated to preserving the environment for coming generations. This includes her support of sustainable practices in the film business as well as her efforts to increase public awareness of renewable energy.

Beyond monetary gifts, De Niro regularly participates in practical initiatives to bring about constructive change in his neighborhood. De Niro sets an example for others by helping at neighborhood charities, taking part in fundraising activities, and utilizing his position to bring attention to important social concerns. These actions encourage others to take action and change the world.

We are reminded of the significant influence one person may have on society when we consider De Niro's business pursuits and charitable activities. In addition to being successful in his own right, De Niro has used his position to inspire others and build a better future for all via hard work, vision, and charity. His legacy is proof of the effectiveness of action, compassion, and the steadfast conviction that each of us can change the world.

We will get into De Niro's personal life and examine the connections and events that have influenced him as a person in the next chapter.

Handling the Personal and Workplace

Many people, like Robert De Niro, are acquainted with the problem of juggling the demands of high-profile work with the complexities of personal life. We examine the fine line De Niro has drawn between his personal and professional commitments in this chapter, illuminating the techniques he uses to manage the intricacies of both domains.

For De Niro, maintaining a healthy balance between his personal and professional lives has been crucial to his success and longevity in the business. He has always placed a higher priority on his family and interpersonal ties than his career pursuits, from his early days as a struggling actor to his current position as a Hollywood heavyweight. He has made time for his loved ones despite the demands of his work, understanding the value of fostering these relationships in the middle of the hectic entertainment world.

De Niro's style is based on a dedication to balance and honesty. He has developed a sense of perspective, seeing that genuine satisfaction comes from a harmonic fusion of professional achievement and personal contentment, as opposed to letting his work take up all of his life. De Niro has shown an unshakeable commitment to keeping his life in balance, whether it's by spending time with his kids or taking pleasure in quiet times away from the limelight.

Of course, it hasn't always been simple to strike this balance. Like every person managing many obligations, De Niro has had difficulties in the past. The challenges he has faced, ranging from demanding production deadlines to the demands of celebrity, have the potential to upset the delicate balance he has laboriously created.

Nevertheless, he has never wavered in his resolve to put his personal life first and has always come up with innovative ways to get over obstacles.

Time management is one of the fundamental techniques De Niro uses to keep her equilibrium. He makes sure that none of the responsibilities in his life take precedence over the other by dividing his time and attention between them. Whether it's planning family vacations during production breaks or allocating specific time for self-care and relaxation, he tackles every day with meaning and a sense of purpose, optimizing output while reducing stress.

Furthermore, De Niro understands the need of candid communication in creating wholesome relationships. He values open and honest communication above all else, whether it's with his kids, his spouse, or his coworkers. This helps to create a climate of trust and understanding. He makes sure

Breaking Barriers, Defying Expectations, and Inspiring Generations

that everyone is aware of his commitments and expectations and that disagreements are resolved amicably by being upfront and honest with those closest to him.

De Niro also values self-care and gives priority to pursuits that feed his body, mind, and spirit. He understands the need of finding time for himself despite the constraints of his hectic schedule, whether it is via meditation, physical activity, or engaging in interests outside of work. He is better able to be totally present and involved in both his personal and professional lives by putting his own health first.

To sum up, Robert De Niro has handled the task of juggling the demands of both his personal and professional lives with elegance and resiliency. By virtue of his adept time management skills, honest communication, and dedication to self-care, he has achieved a state of equilibrium that enables him to flourish in both domains. He sets an inspiring example for how to succeed and find joy in all facets of life by placing a high value on his relationships and overall health in addition to his profession.

Chapter 5

A Durable Legacy of Impact on American Cinema

Robert De Niro has had an enduring impression on the American film business that extends beyond the silver screen. Over the course of his storied career, Robert De Niro has not only given standout performances but also profoundly altered the cinema industry, having an impact on innumerable actors, directors, and spectators.

Through his innovative partnerships with forward-thinking filmmakers and his courageous interpretation of nuanced roles, De Niro has revolutionized the narrative genre, pushing limits and defying expectations. Generations of filmmakers have been inspired by his unwavering pursuit of perfection and dedication to authenticity, which have established a benchmark for filmmaking excellence.

The fact that De Niro can capture the spirit of the characters he plays is among his greatest achievements to American film. Whether he's playing a vicious mafia leader in "The Godfather Part II" or a traumatized Vietnam War veteran in "Taxi Driver," Robert De Niro's performances are distinguished by a depth of passion and an unmatched sincerity that captivates moviegoers in the worlds he creates.

Beyond only his acting career, De Niro has had a significant influence on American film. In reaction to the September 11 attacks, he co-founded the Tribeca Film Festival in 2002 with Jane Rosenthal and Craig Hatkoff, with the intention of reviving the downtown Manhattan area and assisting up-and-coming filmmakers. With time, the festival has developed into one of the most prominent film festivals globally, presenting innovative films and offering a forum for a range of views in the industry.

In addition, De Niro's impact is evident in the many performers and directors he has coached and influenced during his career. From his early partnerships with Martin Scorsese to his more recent cooperation with emerging filmmakers, Robert De Niro has been an inspiration to many looking to get into the business. Aspiring filmmakers have been inspired to follow their talents with steadfast determination by his willingness to take chances and his dedication to creative integrity.

Apart from his creative achievements, De Niro has been a strong supporter of social and political concerns, using his position to create awareness and bring about change. De Niro has never hesitated to use his voice for the greater good, whether he's protesting injustice or promoting environmental preservation. His dedication to changing the world beyond entertainment has been evident via his charitable endeavors, which include his work with the World Food Programme and the Robin Hood Foundation. These initiatives have had a genuine influence on communities all over the globe.

Robert De Niro's impact is still very much felt in modern American film. His corpus of work is proof of the narrative technique's potency and the long-lasting influence of art on society. De Niro's legacy will continue to influence American cinema for years to come, whether it's by inspiring the next generation of directors or mesmerizing viewers with his performances.

To sum up, Robert De Niro had a really enormous influence on American film. He has had a lasting impression on the film business with his performances, activism, and charity. He has changed the way we see movies and encouraged many others to follow their dreams. We are reminded of the transformational power of art and the significant impact one person can have on the world as we consider his enduring legacy.

Breaking Barriers, Defying Expectations, and Inspiring Generations

Effects Internationally

We examine the enormous worldwide impact of Robert De Niro's work in this chapter. Through his innovative performances and unwavering support, Robert De Niro has left a lasting impression on audiences worldwide.

We can tell that De Niro's work has universal themes since he is able to connect with audiences from a wide range of backgrounds. Whether he was playing a damaged Vietnam War veteran in "The Deer Hunter" or a gangster with conflict in "Goodfellas," his performances enthralled audiences worldwide, winning him praise and affection.

Breaking Barriers, Defying Expectations, and Inspiring Generations

In addition to his achievements in movies and television, De Niro's dedication to charity and social problems has cemented his place in history. His engagement in humanitarian endeavors, such as advocating for autism research and aiding Hurricane Sandy victims, has significantly improved people's lives all across the globe.

The creation of the Tribeca Film Festival stands as one of De Niro's greatest gifts to the world. Originally created as a way to bring life to Lower Manhattan after the September 11 attacks, the festival has developed into one of the world's most prestigious international gatherings, drawing moviegoers and directors from all over the world. De Niro has offered a forum for many opinions and viewpoints via the festival, promoting cross-cultural dialogue and creative innovation worldwide.

Moreover, audiences all throughout the globe have responded favorably to De Niro's

Breaking Barriers, Defying Expectations, and Inspiring Generations

campaign for environmental protection. He has utilized his position to spread awareness of important environmental concerns and encourage people to take action in order to save our world for future generations. He is a strong advocate of sustainable living methods.

Beyond his creative pursuits and charitable contributions, De Niro has a significant influence. There is no denying his impact on the international cinema business; actors and directors from all over the globe look up to him as an inspiration and source of respect. De Niro has contributed to the bridging of cultural gaps and the promotion of deeper awareness and respect for various cinematic traditions via his partnerships with foreign filmmakers and involvement in international film festivals.

Furthermore, De Niro has received several awards and recognitions from international governments and organizations as a result of her role as a cultural ambassador. De Niro has represented the greatest of American films on the international scene, winning the respect and admiration of leaders and celebrities everywhere from diplomatic engagements to important award ceremonies.

We conclude by highlighting Robert De Niro's extensive influence and effect on a worldwide level. De Niro has left a lasting impression on the international community via his activism, charity, and performances, touching the lives of people from all over the globe. Thinking back on his legacy serves as a reminder of the ability of art to bridge gaps and bring people together through our common humanity.

Breaking Barriers, Defying Expectations, and Inspiring Generations

Robert De Niro's Political Voice

Robert De Niro has captivated viewers with his unmatched skill on film throughout his lengthy career. He has also used his platform to raise awareness of important social issues. This chapter examines De Niro's entry into the field of political action and advocacy, providing insight into his attempts to have a significant impact outside of the film industry.

Since the beginning of his career, De Niro has not hesitated to utilize his platform to draw attention to urgent social and political concerns. Realizing the influence of his notoriety, he has championed issues that reflect his principles and views, lending his voice to everything from human rights to environmental protection.

Breaking Barriers, Defying Expectations, and Inspiring Generations

The most noteworthy feature of De Niro's advocacy activities is how vocal he is about politics. He has boldly expressed his views on a variety of political topics throughout the years, from immigration reform to gun control. Both acclaim and criticism have been directed at De Niro for his willingness to speak truth to power, but he has not wavered in his resolve to use his position for the benefit of society.

De Niro's political activity has become more urgent in recent years due to the tumultuous political environment. He has become one of the administration's most outspoken critics, publicly denouncing policies and statements that he believes to be divisive or detrimental to the fabric of American society. De Niro has gained notoriety in the resistance movement via speeches, interviews, and social media, mobilizing support for organizations that defend democracy and human freedoms.

Breaking Barriers, Defying Expectations, and Inspiring Generations

In addition to his outspoken support, De Niro has shown his commitment to political candidates and causes who share his beliefs by taking proactive measures. He has supported politicians who support issues including social justice, LGBTQ rights, and healthcare reform by hosting fundraisers, attending campaign events, and using his platform. His participation in politics demonstrates his conviction that citizens have a vital role to play in determining the course of their communities and their nation.

De Niro has actively participated in foreign affairs in addition to his domestic advocacy efforts, supporting causes that advance equality, human rights, and peace. He has visited conflict areas, held meetings with international officials, and utilized his platform to spread awareness of problems like illness, poverty, and displacement brought on by violence. His attempts to promote communication and collaboration

Breaking Barriers, Defying Expectations, and Inspiring Generations

on an international level demonstrate his conviction that mankind is interrelated and that unity is crucial in confronting common problems.

When considering De Niro's political activity, it is important to keep in mind the dangers and difficulties that come with exploiting one's fame to promote change. Because of his vocal positions on some causes, De Niro has encountered criticism, threats, and even boycotts throughout his career. Nevertheless, he hasn't let the possible repercussions of speaking truth to power dissuade him from sticking to his views.

In the end, De Niro's political involvement is a striking reminder that everyone may have a significant effect on the world, regardless of their background or line of work. De Niro is a prime example of the transformational power of advocacy and the lasting legacy that can be formed by ethical leadership and unrelenting dedication to social change. He does this by utilizing his platform to raise vital problems, question the status quo, and inspire others to action. By doing this, he permanently alters the entertainment industry as well as the collective consciousness of society at large.

Getting Past Obstacles

Robert De Niro has encountered several obstacles throughout his long career, both personal and professional. This chapter examines the difficulties that put his fortitude and resolve to the test as well as the methods he used to get through them.

Nailing the constantly shifting Hollywood scene was one of De Niro's toughest obstacles. Even with his extraordinary skill, he had times of doubt and uncertainty and found it difficult to get assignments that suited his creative vision. But instead of giving up on his art, De Niro never wavered in his dedication to it. He didn't let other people's restrictions define him; instead, he looked for chances to push himself creatively.

The strain to uphold his own legacy was another challenge De Niro had to overcome.

It was a hard undertaking for any actor to be expected to perform to the high standards he had set for himself in every new part. Nevertheless, De Niro welcomed the pressure and used it as inspiration rather than letting it immobilize him. He always challenged himself to go above his own standards in his performances, pushing them to new heights.

Apart from the obstacles in his career, De Niro also had personal failures that tested his endurance. He had his fair share of tribulations, from marital problems to health problems to the death of loved ones. Nevertheless, De Niro never wavered in his will to keep going. In spite of hardship, he used his experiences as fuel to keep going on and gained strength from them.

Seeking out the assistance of people in his immediate vicinity was one of De Niro's primary techniques for overcoming obstacles. He surrounded himself with a solid support system of friends, family, and coworkers who helped and supported him through trying times. Their constant encouragement gave De Niro the strength to take on his obstacles head-on with courage and tenacity.

The fact that De Niro was open to changing and growing was another crucial component of his strategy for conquering obstacles. He understood that the acting industry was ever-evolving and that he would have to welcome new challenges and strategies to stay current. In an effort to evolve and innovate, De Niro was never afraid to go outside of his comfort zone, whether it was by trying new things, working with up-and-coming filmmakers, or playing with other genres.

Ultimately, De Niro was able to overcome the obstacles he encountered during his career because of his tenacity and will. Rather than letting his failures define him,

Breaking Barriers, Defying Expectations, and Inspiring Generations

he decided to utilize them as stepping stones to personal development. Through self-truth and unwavering dedication to perfection, De Niro persevered through every obstacle, becoming stronger and more driven than before.

De Niro overcame many challenges and became one of the most admired and beloved performers of his time because of his fortitude, tenacity, and flexibility. His narrative encourages readers to take on their own problems with courage and conviction by serving as a potent reminder of the value of tenacity and bravery in the face of difficulty.

Chapter 6

Fatherhood and Family

Under the bright lights of Hollywood, Robert De Niro's personal life often takes a backseat to his remarkable professional accomplishments. Behind the scenes, however, De Niro is a dedicated family guy in addition to being a talented actor. This chapter explores the nuances of his fathering position and the careful balancing act he does between the pressures of celebrity and fatherhood.

Raising children and navigating the turbulent seas of celebrity provide special obstacles, which De Niro has met with her trademark elegance and tenacity. He has always placed a higher priority on being a father than the demands of his profession, making an effort to offer his kids love, support, and direction even in the middle of Hollywood's glitter and glamor.

De Niro's dedication to teaching his kids ethics, humility, and hard work is the cornerstone of his parenting style. He sets an exemplary example for others, highlighting the value of tenacity and fortitude in the face of difficulty. He teaches them the importance of being genuine and keeping loyal to oneself in the face of attention and recognition via his deeds.

But it's not easy to juggle celebrity with fatherhood, and De Niro has had to make some compromises along the way. He has to come up with inventive methods to maintain a relationship with his kids since his hectic schedule often requires him to spend long stretches of time away from home. Even yet, he continues to be a

Breaking Barriers, Defying Expectations, and Inspiring Generations

constant in their lives, making an effort to attend milestones like birthdays and school functions.

The value of striking a balance in life is among the most important things De Niro teaches his kids. By encouraging them to follow their hobbies and passions away from the limelight, he helps them develop a feeling of self-reliance and autonomy. De Niro wants to give his kids the skills they need to deal with the challenges of celebrity and find contentment in all facets of their life by establishing this balance in them at a young age.

But shielding his kids from the demands and attention that come with being the famous actor's child is perhaps the hardest thing De Niro has to do as a public parent. By fostering a secure and supportive atmosphere, he hopes to protect kids from the unseen gaze of the media and the expectations of others.

Breaking Barriers, Defying Expectations, and Inspiring Generations

De Niro enjoys the straightforward joys of family life and treasures the times he spends with his kids despite the difficulties. He cherishes the time he spends with his kids, knowing that these are the best indicators of his success as a parent, whether it's a peaceful supper at home or a weekend trip.

In the end, De Niro's fathering journey serves as a monument to the strength of commitment, love, and sacrifice. It takes a delicate dance to balance stardom and fatherhood, but De Niro does it with unshakeable passion and love. He shows by his deeds that while celebrity may come and go, a parent-child relationship lasts a lifetime.

We learn more about the man behind the classic roles as we examine De Niro's position as a parent. The principles that have guided him throughout his life—integrity, fortitude, and a profound feeling of love and compassion—are reflected in his dedication to his kids. De Niro reminds us that the love and support we offer to our children is the best legacy we can leave behind in a society that frequently values celebrity and riches above all else.

Breaking Barriers, Defying Expectations, and Inspiring Generations

Examining Various Genres

The acting versatility of Robert De Niro is remarkable. He has bravely taken on a broad range of parts across several genres over his distinguished career, demonstrating his unmatched brilliance and versatility. This chapter takes us on a tour of De Niro's varied filmography, highlighting the wide range of characters he has portrayed and the genres he has skillfully moved between.

De Niro has shown to have a unique capacity to embody characters with depth and sincerity in a variety of genres, including grim dramas and loud comedies. His early parts in movies like "Taxi Driver" and "Mean Streets" made him a formidable presence in the world of dramatic and passionate storytelling. He took on parts in comedies like "Meet the Parents" and "Analyze This," where he demonstrated his perfect timing and comic skills, while he continued to grow as an actor.

De Niro's willingness to take chances and push himself with characters that push the limits of traditional narrative is one of his most enduring professional traits. In "The Deer Hunter," he showed that he could handle difficult and emotionally taxing material by giving a melancholic picture of a Vietnam War veteran struggling with the pain of his experiences. Similar to this, he played a terrifying and mentally unstable guy in "Cape Fear," which had viewers on the edge of their seats.

Perhaps the most notable example of De Niro's adaptability is his work with renowned filmmaker Martin Scorsese. In each of these films, De Niro has completely transformed himself, immersing himself in the worlds of his characters and bringing

Breaking Barriers, Defying Expectations, and Inspiring Generations

them to life with an unmatched depth and authenticity. Together, they have explored a wide range of genres, from crime dramas like "Goodfellas" and "The Irishman" to period pieces like "The Age of Innocence."

However, De Niro's abilities go beyond the conventional film industry. He has been pushing the limits of his trade in recent years, acting in films like "Silver Linings Playbook" and "Joker," where he has stepped into uncharted areas. He has shown in these movies that he is prepared to play unusual parts and tackle the complexity of the human condition in fresh and creative ways.

The most amazing things about De Niro's career have been his ability to break stereotypes and transcend genre. Whether portraying a loving father figure, a tortured war veteran, or a hardened mobster, De Niro tackles every part with the same degree of devotion and passion, giving every

Breaking Barriers, Defying Expectations, and Inspiring Generations

performance authenticity and total immersion in the movie's universe.

Together with his work in film, De Niro has shown his abilities as a producer and director. Films such as "A Bronx Tale" and "The Good Shepherd" highlight his skill in both areas. His reputation as one of the best performers of his time has been cemented by the praise and acclaim that his many abilities have brought him from both critics and viewers.

We are reminded of the depth and breadth of De Niro's ability as well as the influence he has had on the film industry as we examine the variety of parts he has played throughout his career. De Niro has irrevocably impacted every genre he has worked in, from gripping dramas to belly-laughing comedy, and his legacy will inspire and enthrall viewers for many years to come.

Evolution and Adaptability for a Long-Term Career

Robert De Niro's long career is evidence of his extraordinary flexibility and continuous development as an actor. De Niro has not only survived but flourished in a field notorious for its ephemeral nature and constantly shifting fashions, staying revered and relevant for several decades.

De Niro's capacity for change and taking on new challenges has been a major contributor to his long-term success. De Niro has continuously shown a willingness to push himself past his comfort zone, from his early days as a method actor who threw himself completely into his roles to his later years where he has moved between genres with ease.

Breaking Barriers, Defying Expectations, and Inspiring Generations

De Niro has demonstrated incredible versatility throughout his career, moving between dramatic roles, comedic roles, and all in between with ease. With roles in both serious dramas like "Taxi Driver" and "Raging Bull" as well as lighter comedies like "Meet the Parents" and "Silver Linings Playbook," De Niro's creative versatility is unmatched. His ability to authentically and deeply embody a broad range of roles has garnered him tremendous praise and solidified his place among the best performers of his day.

Apart from his adeptness as an actor, De Niro has also shown a strong sense of flexibility in maneuvering through the constantly evolving film business. De Niro has welcomed these developments as technology has developed and new narrative media have appeared. He has experimented with many formats and platforms to reach people in fresh and creative ways.

Breaking Barriers, Defying Expectations, and Inspiring Generations

Virtual reality filming is one instance of De Niro's openness to embracing new technology. De Niro has been working with filmmakers in recent years to produce realistic virtual reality experiences that let viewers enter the worlds of his movies like never before. De Niro has made sure that his work is engaging and relevant in an increasingly digital environment by embracing new technology.

In addition to his work in film, De Niro has shown flexibility in his approach to his job in general. As he's gotten older, he's sought chances outside of performing, such as producing and directing, and taken on new challenges. His participation in events like the Tribeca Film Festival and "A Bronx Tale" demonstrates his dedication to fostering new talent and enhancing the film industry.

De Niro's commitment to his work has not wavered despite time and the changes that it always brings. He keeps looking for parts that would test his abilities as an actor and stretch the limits of his imagination. Whether he's portraying a nasty mobster or a charming grandpa, De Niro delivers the same level of energy and devotion to every performance, ensuring that his work continues to fascinate audiences across the globe.

In conclusion, Robert De Niro's ability to continue a lengthy and successful career in Hollywood is a testimonial to his versatility and constant improvement as an actor. By accepting new challenges, pushing himself artistically, and staying loyal to his profession, De Niro has secured his place as a real cinematic legend. As he continues to captivate audiences with his brilliance and range, one thing is clear: Robert De Niro's legacy will survive for centuries to come.

Molding the Next Generation

Beyond the roles he plays on screen, Robert De Niro's impact is felt deeply in the film business and has a lasting impression on aspiring actors and directors worldwide. This chapter examines De Niro's influence on the next artistic generations as well as his lasting significance as a teacher and inspiration.

De Niro has mentored up-and-coming musicians throughout his career, using his vast knowledge and expertise to help shape the next generation of performers. His devotion to sharing his knowledge with others, whether via official mentoring programs or unofficial advice on set, demonstrates his devotion to the acting trade.

By his participation in the Tribeca Film Festival, De Niro has influenced future generations in one of the most important ways. The festival was established in 2002 with the intention of reviving Lower Manhattan after the 9/11 attacks. Since then, it has developed into a prestigious venue for exhibiting independent film and assisting up-and-coming directors. The success of the festival has been greatly attributed to De Niro's enthusiasm for encouraging innovation and giving budding filmmakers chances, and audiences find inspiration in his presence.

Throughout his career, De Niro has assumed mentoring duties in a variety of positions in addition to his work with the Tribeca Film Festival. He is renowned for his generosity in giving his knowledge and providing direction to those who want it, whether he is

Breaking Barriers, Defying Expectations, and Inspiring Generations

working with young actors on set or advising upcoming filmmakers. His mentoring is defined by a blend of steadfast support and tough love, pushing budding artists to go outside of their comfort zones and giving them the assistance they need to be successful.

Beyond his involvement in mentoring programs and film festivals, De Niro will continue to have an effect on next generations. Aspiring actors may learn a lot from his unwavering devotion to authenticity and skill, which serves as a brilliant example of the value of being true to oneself and approaching work with integrity. His ability to portray a wide range of characters with subtlety and depth has motivated a great number of aspiring actors to pursue greatness and believe in the transformational potential of acting.

Additionally, De Niro's courage to try new things and take on unusual parts has opened

Breaking Barriers, Defying Expectations, and Inspiring Generations

doors for more diversity and representation in the film industry. He has made it possible for performers from various backgrounds to follow their goals and share their tales on film by dispelling myths and tearing down obstacles. His backing of marginalized voices and his push for diversity have had a significant influence on the business, influencing the tales and narratives that are portrayed.

We are reminded of the value of giving back to the community and paying it forward when we consider how influential De Niro was in influencing the careers of upcoming artists. His dedication to developing up-and-coming artists and giving others the chance to thrive is evidence of his kindness and faith in the transformational potential of art. De Niro reminds us that true greatness lies in the capacity to inspire and uplift others, leaving a legacy that extends far beyond the boundaries of the silver

Breaking Barriers, Defying Expectations, and Inspiring Generations

screen. In a world where success is often measured by individual achievements.

Chapter 7

Character Development as an Art

Actors and viewers alike hold the skill of bringing a character to life in the role with such reverence. Robert De Niro views his artistry as a painstaking process of immersion, exploration, and transformation that goes far beyond simple performance.

De Niro's approach is centered on an unwavering dedication to authenticity. He doesn't just play characters; he becomes them, fully engrossing himself in their mannerisms, motivations, and emotions with a level of comprehension that is immersive and captivating. Whether he's playing the erratic Travis Bickle in "Taxi Driver" or the moody Vito Corleone in "The

Godfather Part II," De Niro captures the emotions of his characters viscerally and draws them into the worlds he expertly crafts.

De Niro pays great attention to detail, which is one of the characteristics that define his character development. He makes every effort to be authentic, paying attention to even the smallest details in speech and movement. He fully immerses himself in the world of his characters, learning about their upbringing, observing their behaviors, and even taking on their dialects and accents. His performances come to life thanks to this meticulous attention to detail, which raises them above the level of simple acting to that of true art.

De Niro's strategy also revolves on his daring and willingness to go against the grain of traditional narrative. Taking on complicated or contentious personalities, he is not hesitant to go deeply into his subjects' minds to reveal the hidden realities. This bold attitude has resulted in some of his most legendary performances, compelling viewers to face hard realities and igniting debates that echo long after the credits roll.

But arguably the most astonishing part of De Niro's character development is his ability to discover empathy in even the most imperfect or vile people. He refuses to criticize or condemn his subjects, instead seeks to understand the reasons and events that have molded them. This sensitivity seeps through in his performances, letting viewers to identify with people who may otherwise be considered as irredeemable.

At the core of De Niro's approach to character development is a genuine appreciation for the craft of acting. He regards each position as a chance for development and discovery, tackling each new endeavor with humility and an open mind. He engages extensively with directors,

Breaking Barriers, Defying Expectations, and Inspiring Generations

writers, and other actors, pulling inspiration from their views and experiences to influence his own performance. It is this collaborative mentality that has resulted in some of his most memorable collaborations and breakthrough performances.

Ultimately, De Niro's approach to character development is a tribute to his enthusiasm for his job and his persistent devotion to perfection. Through painstaking study, bold investigation, and a strong appreciation for the art of acting, he has built a body of work that stands as a tribute to the power of narrative and the lasting influence of outstanding performances.

As we reflect on De Niro's journey through the prism of character development, we are reminded of the transformational power of art and the capacity of great performers to take us to places both real and imaginary. In the hands of a maestro like Robert De Niro, character development becomes not simply a procedure, but a voyage of discovery, empathy, and self-expression.

Collaboration with Masterful Directors

In addition to his extraordinary skill, Robert De Niro's career is notable for his partnerships with some of the greatest filmmakers in movie history. Over the course of his storied career, De Niro has had the honor of collaborating with avant-garde directors who push the envelope of narrative and bring out the best in their performers.

One such cooperation that has lasted for many years and produced some of the most recognizable movies in movie history is with Martin Scorsese. From their first working together on "Mean Streets" to their most recent project, "The Irishman," De Niro and Scorsese have established a creative

Breaking Barriers, Defying Expectations, and Inspiring Generations

chemistry that is unmatched in the film industry.

Apart from his association with Scorsese, De Niro has furthermore cooperated with other renowned filmmakers, each of whom has contributed their own perspective. Michael Mann, Brian De Palma, and Francis Ford Coppola are just a few of the directors who have acknowledged De Niro's extraordinary skill and worked to use it to further their own creative goals.

Coppola's "The Godfather Part II" gave De Niro one of his most famous parts, emulating the youthful Vito Corleone with a level of delicacy and depth that won him both his first Academy Award and critical praise. De Palma's "The Untouchables" demonstrated De Niro's flexibility by having him play legendary mobster Al Capone with a combination of terror and charm. Additionally, Mann's "Heat" featured De

Breaking Barriers, Defying Expectations, and Inspiring Generations

Niro and fellow A-list actor Al Pacino in an exciting cat-and-mouse battle that had viewers gripped from start to finish.

The regard and appreciation that De Niro and the filmmakers he collaborates with have for one another is what distinguishes these partnerships. Every filmmaker has his own aesthetic and point of view, which pushes De Niro to stretch his artistic boundaries and discover new heights as an actor. In exchange, De Niro offers his unmatched devotion to the art and his astonishingly high degree of sincerity while playing characters.

The long-lasting influence De Niro's partnerships with these exceptional filmmakers have had on the film industry, however, may be their most noteworthy feature. Not only are movies like "Taxi Driver" and "Raging Bull" regarded highly for their artistic qualities, but they have also influenced our perceptions of narrative and filmmaking. They established a bar of quality that is being met today, inspiring a new generation of performers and filmmakers.

One aspect of De Niro's career that hasn't changed is his commitment to working with the greatest in the industry. Knowing that the magic of film is derived from teamwork, De Niro tackles every partnership with the same zeal and dedication, regardless of whether he is collaborating with a seasoned veteran or a budding star.

In summary, Robert De Niro's partnerships with exceptional filmmakers have shaped his career and left a lasting impression on the film industry. Through these collaborations, De Niro has improved both his own work and the advancement of cinema as an art form. We can only imagine the magic that will result from his future partnerships as audiences remain enthralled with his performances.

Outstanding Acts of the Twenty-First Century

Robert De Niro entered a new phase of his career at the beginning of the twenty-first century, one that was characterized by his unwavering dedication to his work and his readiness to take on a range of parts in a number of genres. De Niro continued to be a dependable presence on the silver screen as audiences transitioned into the digital era, giving captivating performances that enthralled audiences and cemented his reputation as one of the best performers of his time.

De Niro's role of Jack Byrnes in the comedy "Meet the Parents" (2000) and its sequels is one of the most memorable performances of the twenty-first century. Alongside Ben

Stiller, De Niro displayed his comic skills in this part, giving the character of a protective father suspicious of his daughter's suitor complexity and subtlety. Audiences were captivated by his flawless timing and heartfelt comedy, which demonstrated that his skill was not limited to serious parts.

In 2006, De Niro portrayed Max Cady in Martin Scorsese's psychological thriller "Cape Fear," reimagining the iconic role previously played by Robert Mitchum. De Niro embodied the essence of pure evil with chilling precision and brought a menacing intensity to the role. He received praise from critics for his depiction of the resentful ex-convict, which helped him further establish his standing as a master of his trade.

In the world of indie film, De Niro persisted in pushing limits and testing his acting abilities. His role in the 2012 film "Silver Linings Playbook" was that of Pat Solitano

Breaking Barriers, Defying Expectations, and Inspiring Generations

Sr., a kind but imperfect father who finds it difficult to help his son deal with mental illness. De Niro's portrayal demonstrated his capacity to emote depth and sensitivity in even the most subdued parts, earning him a nomination for the Academy Award for Best Supporting Actor.

In the film "Joy" (2015), directed by David O. Russell, De Niro reprised his role as Rudy Mangano, the kind father of Jennifer Lawrence's driven businesswoman. Audiences responded favorably to his depiction of an industrious businessman struggling with the complexity of family relationships, and he was praised for his subtle yet impactful performance.

De Niro and Martin Scorsese collaborated again on "The Irishman" (2019), a massive epic that took place over many decades. In the role of Frank Sheeran, the title character, De Niro gave a performance that defined his career and demonstrated the breadth of his acting abilities. De Niro gave Sheeran a rich and nuanced portrayal, garnering critical praise and several nominations for awards, spanning the hitman's early years to his senior years as he struggled with shame and regret.

Robert De Niro's unmatched brilliance and adaptability have kept him captivating audiences far into the twenty-first century. De Niro continues to be a major player in the film industry, whether she is bringing laughter to comedies, delving into the depths of the human mind in thrillers, or interpreting complicated characters in tragedies.

We are reminded of the timeless quality of his genius and the lasting effect of his work as we think back on his unforgettable performances in the twenty-first century. Generations of actors and filmmakers have been inspired to pursue careers in acting

Breaking Barriers, Defying Expectations, and Inspiring Generations

and cinema by De Niro's constant pushing of the limits of his art with each new role.

One thing never changes in the ever-evolving world of film: Robert De Niro's indisputable genius. We are optimistic that he will continue to captivate viewers and make a lasting impression on the film industry as we impatiently await the next chapter in his illustrious career.

Chapter 8

Acquiring Knowledge from a Living Myth

Robert De Niro is one of the most iconic personalities in the constantly changing world of film. It is clear that there is much to learn from his experiences when we consider his illustrious career and ongoing impact. This chapter goes into the priceless lessons that may be drawn from the life and career of this giant of film.

De Niro's commitment to his work is among its most remarkable features. He has continuously shown a dedication to perfection over his decades-long career in Hollywood, challenging himself to new heights with each part. De Niro tackles every role with the same seriousness and accuracy, whether he's taking on the persona of a larger-than-life crime leader or delving into the mind of a tormented protagonist.

His unrelenting commitment to his profession serves as a potent reminder of the value of persistence and hard effort. De Niro has never faltered in his quest of creative greatness, despite the difficulties he has encountered. His dedication to the acting trade is shown by his willingness to invest the time and energy required to truly embody his roles.

Apart from his unwavering commitment to his profession, De Niro is renowned for his adaptability as an actor. He's repeatedly shown that he can handle any genre with ease, whether it's breezy comedies or heavy tragedies. He has been able to connect with audiences of all ages because of his flexibility, which has also allowed him to explore a broad variety of roles.

Breaking Barriers, Defying Expectations, and Inspiring Generations

De Niro's ability to change with the times is one of his most lasting professional traits. With his subtle performances and unwavering realism, De Niro has managed to engage audiences for years on end, something that many aging actors find difficult to do. He gives his roles an intensity and nuance that is unrivaled in the business, whether he is playing a charming grandpa or a tortured war veteran.

Most crucial, however, is that De Niro's career is a potent illustration of the influence one person can have on a whole industry. His avant-garde style of filming and ground-breaking performances have encouraged a great deal of performers and filmmakers to push the limits of their medium. From indie films to high-end blockbusters, his impact can be seen everywhere in the film industry.

Breaking Barriers, Defying Expectations, and Inspiring Generations

It's evident that Robert De Niro's influence goes far beyond the silver screen when we consider the lessons that may be drawn from his career. Aspiring artists worldwide may find encouragement in his steadfast commitment to his work, his adaptability as an actor, and his capacity to change with the times. There's a lot to learn from the life and career of this living classic, whether you're an actor, director, or just a movie buff.

Finally, for those who are open to listening, Robert De Niro's career has a plethora of lessons to teach. Aspiring artists may learn a lot from his example, from his commitment to his profession to his ability to change with the times. Let's draw inspiration from the life and work of this incredible person as we continue to navigate the always shifting film industry and endeavor to leave our own imprint.

Robert De Niro's Enduring Impact

As our journey through the life and career of a cinematic giant comes to a conclusion, we find ourselves thinking back on Robert De Niro's lasting legacy. It is very evident that his influence goes far beyond the silver screen as we sift through the rich tapestry of his experiences and accomplishments.

We have followed the development of a man whose name has come to represent quality and creativity in the film industry via the pages of this book. De Niro's story, from his modest origins on the streets of New York City to his quick ascent to worldwide recognition, is proof of the transformational power of skill, tenacity, and unflinching commitment.

De Niro's dedication to sincerity and integrity in his work is what defines his

Breaking Barriers, Defying Expectations, and Inspiring Generations

legacy. Whether he's playing the tough toughness of Travis Bickle in "Taxi Driver" or the heartbreaking gullibility of Vito Corleone in "The Godfather Part II," De Niro brings an unmatched depth and subtlety to every character. Generations of performers and filmmakers are still motivated by his level of perfection in craft skill.

However, De Niro's impact goes well beyond his cinematic roles. His business ventures, including starting the Tribeca Film Festival, have given up-and-coming talent a stage and created a feeling of industry community. His advocacy activity demonstrates a strong dedication to leveraging his position to bring about good change, whether it is by promoting environmental causes or increasing public awareness of social concerns.

It is clear that De Niro's influence extends beyond the entertainment industry when we

Breaking Barriers, Defying Expectations, and Inspiring Generations

consider the lessons that may be drawn from his path. For those who desire to be great, his fortitude in the face of difficulty, his willingness to take chances and push the envelope, and his unshakable commitment to his art serve as a light of inspiration.

De Niro's unwavering devotion to his beliefs reminds us of the lasting force of honesty and integrity in a society too frequently marked by uncertainty and instability. Whether it is by refusing to play characters that conform to social standards or by raising his voice in support of issues that are personal to him, De Niro never fails to motivate us to stand up for what we believe in and pursue greatness in everything that we do.

Let's take the timeless lessons from Robert De Niro's life and profession with us as we say goodbye to the pages of this book. Let's embrace the spirit of tenacity, resolve, and unflinching commitment that has characterized his path. And let us keep drawing inspiration from his legacy as we go forth on our own paths to success.

Let us conclude by honoring Robert De Niro's enduring legacy as a film icon whose influence will continue to be felt for many years to come.

Food for thought

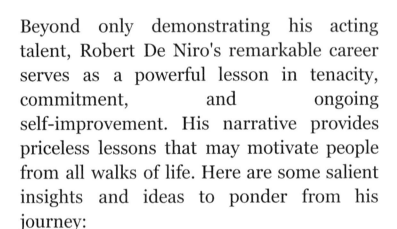

Beyond only demonstrating his acting talent, Robert De Niro's remarkable career serves as a powerful lesson in tenacity, commitment, and ongoing self-improvement. His narrative provides priceless lessons that may motivate people from all walks of life. Here are some salient insights and ideas to ponder from his journey:

1. Dedicated to the Craft

Robert De Niro is well known for his careful planning and commitment to his performances. His devotion to realism is unmatched, whether it's picking up Sicilian for "The Godfather Part II" or putting on a lot of weight for "Raging Bull." This degree of commitment teaches us the value of putting our all into every endeavor we undertake. Hard labor, meticulous attention to detail, and an unwavering quest of progress are often the results of excellence.

2. Adopting Flexibility

De Niro has performed a broad spectrum of characters throughout his career, from comic to very somber ones. This adaptability emphasizes how important it is to be flexible and ready to push oneself beyond one's comfort zone. Diversifying our skill set and taking on new challenges may open up new doors for development and opportunity.

3. Extended Partnerships

Some of the most recognizable movies in history have been made because of De Niro's partnerships with filmmakers like Martin Scorsese. These alliances highlight the value of enduring cooperation and mutual trust.

Developing solid business ties may boost innovation and result in long-term success.

4. Keeping Going Despite Rejection

Early in his career, De Niro experienced a lot of rejection and disappointment. Still, he persisted, always improving his skill and looking for chances to show off his abilities. This tenacity serves as a potent reminder that obstacles are not signs of failure but rather of opportunities for growth and accomplishment. For one to overcome barriers, persistence and the capacity to maintain focus on long-term objectives are essential.

5. Mentoring's Effect

Mentors such as Stella Adler and Lee Strasberg had a big impact on De Niro's career. Their advice influenced the way he approached acting. This emphasizes how crucial it is to look for mentoring and pick up knowledge from those with greater expertise. Mentors may provide insightful advice, encouragement, and support that can greatly aid in our professional trip navigation.

6. Juggling Life at Home and at Work

De Niro has succeeded in striking a balance between his personal and professional lives in spite of his notoriety. In addition to being a devoted parent, he has launched many businesses, including the Tribeca Film Festival. Maintaining long-term prosperity and wellbeing requires this balance. It serves as a reminder that achieving professional success and finding personal contentment are not mutually incompatible but rather may enhance one another.

7. Making Use of Fame for Good

De Niro is a perfect example of how one may utilize power for good by utilizing it to promote social and political concerns. This shows us how important it is to have social responsibility and use our achievements to change the world for the better.

8. Ongoing Education and Adjustment

De Niro has shown a desire to change and grow during his career. Even after experiencing great success, he keeps pushing himself by taking on new parts and directing endeavors. This attitude of continual learning is essential in a world that is changing quickly. We may stay involved and relevant in both our personal and professional lives by continuing to be inquisitive and receptive to new things.

9. Sincerity and Truthfulness

De Niro has gained respect and adoration for being genuine both on and off film. Developing a lasting legacy requires being loyal to oneself and upholding honesty.

Since authenticity promotes connection and trust, it deepens the significance of both our personal and professional relationships.

10. Motivating Next Generations

Numerous young actors and artists have been influenced by De Niro via his career and public persona. His story demonstrates that skill, diligence, and persistence can lead to success. We may encourage next generations to follow their aspirations by telling our tales and lending a helping hand to others.

Acknowledgement

This book seeks to celebrate the memory of a man whose passion and devotion have inspired millions.

My family and friends have always believed in our idea, and for that I am really thankful. Your support has been very helpful.

A special thanks goes to the designers, and researchers who put in many hours to make this book a reality. Your knowledge and dedication have greatly influenced this effort.

I want to thank all of the readers for showing interest in my work. This project is only worthwhile because of your support.

I respectfully ask that you write a *review* of *"Breaking Barriers, Defying Expectations, and Inspiring Generations: The Robert De Niro Story"* if it has inspired you. In order for others to read the book and benefit from Robert De Niro's amazing experience, your opinions are very important.

We are grateful that you shared Robert De Niro's story and its inspirational and educational value with others by traveling with us.

Get your book now, write a review, and keep being inspired by one of the greatest icons in Hollywood history. Your input and assistance are much valued.

Printed in Great Britain
by Amazon